The Internet and Social Welfare Policy

A Supplement to

American Social Welfare Policy
A Pluralist Approach

Howard Jacob Karger
University of Houston

and

David Stoesz
Virginia Commonwealth University

Allyn and Bacon
Boston London Toronto Sydney Tokyo Singapore

ISBN 0-205-35445-9

Printed in the United States of America

10 9 8 7 6 5 4 3   03

CONTENTS

INTRODUCTION:

The Internet and Social Welfare Policy

his supplement is designed to help students and others become acquainted with the principles of

e Internet (Net) and its various parts, including the World Wide Web (WWW), e-mail, Listserv

d USENET Newsgroups. Also designed to provide some useful tips on hardware and software

oices, this supplement addresses how to navigate and use the Net, including the conventions

d protocols expected of users. Lastly, this supplement includes a sample of policy-oriented

eb sites and a glossary of terms useful for understanding the Internet and its related functions.

Before turning to this supplement, some *caveats* are in order. First, this supplement is not

tended as a step-by-step introduction to Internet functions such as the WWW, e-mail, Listservs,

wsgroups, Telnet and so forth. This can be found in Howard Jacob Karger and Joanne Levine's

he Ultimate Guide to Internet and Technology for the Human Services (Longman, 1999).

ritten from a hands-on perspective, *The Ultimate Guide* is designed to examine the practical

es and problems (i.e., confidentiality, ethics, etc.) of the Internet for human service

ofessionals. Written in a user-friendly way, *The Ultimate Guide* is designed for the novice,

termediate and advanced user who wants to better utilize Internet technology. Recognizing that

any human service professionals are often "high touch" and "low tech," the book begins with

 "consumer-based information approach" to Internet technology and then moves on to a

nformation-based producer approach." In short, *The Ultimate Guide* takes the reader through

e process of preparing for, getting on, and using the Internet. It does this by providing a step-

y-step guide to Internet functions that are the most relevant to human services such as Web browsing, e-mail, Listservs, newsgroups and Telnet. It ends with a step-by-step explanation on how to design and publish a Web page.

Secondly, because events are changing so rapidly, some of the software, hardware and Internet sites discussed here will be outdated even before this supplement is printed. Other, newer, perhaps better, software packages and Web sites will have been created in the meantim For instance, the first version of this supplement was written in the summer of 1996. Since the both Netscape and Microsoft have come out with new versions of their Web browsers. In addition, the 33.6 KBPS modem that was state-of-the-art in 1996 has been replaced by the fast 56.6 KBPS modem. In the next two years it is likely that the cable modem (i.e., which uses the same cable as cable television) will replace standalone modems. Internet technology is moving a brisk pace.

Thirdly, the hardware and software options discussed here are presented as a brief guide not a definitive source for information. Students wanting to purchase hardware or software should look to other, more complete sources of information which are found in consumer guide computer magazines, and so forth. Fourthly, the hardware and software discussed here are base on IBM-compatible computers. This is not to suggest that these computers are superior to Appl products. They are not. Rather, IBM compatible computers account for about 90 percent of the computer market, and therefore — for better or worse — they are the most common choice of computer buyers. Fifthly, this supplement examines graphical Internet access through the Microsoft (MS) Windows operating system. This is not meant to endorse MS Windows; instea it acknowledges that the overwhelming majority of novice and intermediate users choose MS indows as their graphical operating system. While other operating systems may be as good or

tter than MS Windows, they are used primarily by advanced users.

WHAT IS THE INTERNET?

oing beyond the hype of "superhighways" and "information revolutions," the Internet is a

ghly misunderstood part of modern information/communications technology. In simple terms,

e Internet is a global network of millions of computers linked together by satellites and phone

1es that communicate in a common language. Similar to the international telephone system, no

1e owns or controls the Internet. This large network of interconnected computers is regularly

ccessed by well over thirty million people worldwide.

The new communication and information technologies discussed in this supplement are

1anging the way people work, including social workers and policy analysts. While these new

chnologies, including the Internet, promise untold numbers of people easy access to vast

1nounts of information, they are not without problems. For one, the speed of this revolution has

ft many people standing outside of the technological loop. Many of these people make up the

1me vulnerable populations that social workers have long been concerned with — the elderly,

1inorities, the poor, and those living in low-income rural areas. Understanding and accessing the

2w communication and information technologies will prove to be a key factor in determining

1e structure of social classes in the future. Children in families able to purchase the hardware,

1ftware, and Internet services needed to utilize this technology will be advantaged by their

1ility to grasp the new information technology and the logic behind it. Conversely, unless public schools embark on an aggressive strategy to teach *all* children these skills, poor children risk being left out of the technological loop.

Contrary to the belief of some of the early computer pioneers, including Apple founder Steven Jobs, the new computer technologies do not necessarily lead to greater democracy, a better-informed polity or a fairer society. In fact, these new technologies may help further underscore the primacy of private over public life. For example, in contrast to attending lectures engaging others in dynamic and direct encounters, meeting people face-to-face with similar interests, and having a rich social interaction with the external world, the new information/communication technologies — including the Internet — can reinforce a sense of private space. While it may be more comfortable for many people to engage the outside world in the comfort of their office or living room, the interaction is usually less powerful and transformative than a direct encounter. Using a disembodied means of communication (i.e., not having to be physically present) to engage the world can lead to greater alienation for significant numbers of people.

Given these and other problems, why should anyone bother to learn to use the Internet? The simple answer is that not everyone needs to use the Net. For example, if you don't know anyone who is on e-mail, or have decided that you don't want to spend time in cyberspace, then you probably don't need the Internet. If you prefer to find the information you need by going to the library and reading books, journals, and magazines instead of searching through cyberspace, you probably don't need the Net. On the other hand, the competent practice of social work in the modern world is increasingly becoming dependent on some form of technological familiarity.

Moreover, these new information/communication technologies can help people understand the smallness and interconnectedness of our world. On balance, there are clearly important trade-offs to be made in accommodating to any new technology, especially those that narrow rather than expand our physical space. For some people, the Net offers important opportunities to uncover information, make connections with people who have similar interests, and expand their horizons.

HOW CAN THE NET HELP ME?

The Internet has become an important source for social policy research and for the preparation of term papers and professional articles. Web sites can be rich in information and contain data that is more current than professional journals. Specifically, there is a long lag time in professional journals (often a year and sometimes two) between when an article is submitted and when it is finally published. Information in these journals is by nature dated. On the other hand, Web sites can be updated with new information on a daily basis, if needed. The up-to-the-minute nature of Web sites make them a popular venue for social policy researchers. The appeal of Web research also includes the ease of finding, sorting and copying current information from the Internet.

Despite the Internet's positive benefits for research, certain *caveats* are in order. First, reports and information appearing on the Internet are frequently not reviewed for accuracy by peer reviewers. For example, an article appearing in a professional journal usually undergoes a blind review by two peer reviewers. Part of this review is to ascertain the accuracy of the manuscript. Reputable organizations also check the accuracy of documents posted on their Web page. On the other hand, some organizations may simply post opinions that masquerade as facts.

In fact, the Web is known for spreading rumors that have no basis in fact. Moreover, some Web sites will post false information that is essentially propaganda. Information coming from non-mainstream Web sites should be checked for accuracy and the reliability of the sources. In addition, the Internet provides a rife medium for plagiarism. Large documents can be cut and pasted into word processors and credits can be claimed by anyone accessing that page. This is especially true since unlike print mediums, those found on Web sites are rarely copyrighted. Students should be careful not to inadvertently spread plagiarized documents. Several examples help illustrate the usefulness of the Internet.

1. As students of social work, you are responsible for writing term papers and doing other kinds of research. Your research efforts on these projects can take a great deal of time an may require many trips to the library, phone calls to government offices to find data, and difficulties in locating the latest research studies. The Internet make these tasks easier by allowing you to find the latest government data online (thereby saving us trips to the library), by locating current research studies directly at the source and by accessing libra materials (including journal articles) from home.

2. Most of you correspond with friends and family, some of them abroad. Snail mail (surface mail) can take days to arrive and phone calls can be expensive. If you correspon with friends or family in developing countries, letters can sometimes take weeks or even months to arrive. There is also no guarantee that they will actually arrive at their destination. Collaboration with friends and families in these countries can be difficult. E-mail helps solves the problem. E-mail letters within the U.S. and Canada often arrive in

seconds or minutes rather than days. Documents can be attached to those letters and written work can go back and forth electronically.

Students have a wide range of responsibilities, one of which is to keep up with current events. You can do this by purchasing a large number of newspapers and magazines. Alternatively, you can access the various newspapers and magazines online, including *The New York Times*, *The Washington Post* and a large number of magazines spanning the political continuum. Although the Internet is not yet a substitute for printed materials, it is a good complement to them. The Internet also allows you to find fast-breaking news not yet printed in the newspapers. Lastly, subscriptions to various professional Listservs allow you to keep up with debates and new ideas in the social work field.

The father of a close friend had become seriously ill. Admitted into intensive care, it was clear that if he survived, he would require considerable aftercare. Sarah, a social worker in a large northeastern hospital, had used all of her sick days, vacation days and personal leave time caring for her father's previous illnesses. If she took off time again, she would likely be fired. Meanwhile, her father lay seriously ill and every minute counted. After some discussion we realized that she *might* be eligible for the Family Medical Leave Act (FMLA), a bill that had then been recently passed by Congress. Traveling to the library or phoning the federal government for details on the FMLA would have been too time-consuming. Instead, we logged on to the Internet and in less than thirty minutes had downloaded and printed the information on the FMLA. Finding that she was eligible, Sarah immediately made her way to human resources (with the documents in hand) and asked that she be approved for an FMLA leave — which guaranteed her job upon her return and maintained her benefits during the leave. The leave was granted and within an hour Sarah was on her way to her father's hospital room. He survived and she took care of him until he recovered. Sarah's job was waiting.

WHAT'S ON THE NET?

The Internet offers myriad opportunities for information and entertainment:

- There are volumes of material from governmental agencies such as the Departments of Health and Human Services, Transportation, Commerce, Housing and Urban Development. Congress, the Centers for Disease Control, and others are also online.

- Information is posted online from a variety of think-tanks and policy institutes representing the continuum of American political thought.

- The Internet contains magazines such as *Time and Newsweek* and portions of newspaper like the *New York Times, The Washington Post* and the *Wall Street Journal.* There are a variety of publications from around the world, including foreign newspapers and magazines.

- The Internet contains discussion groups (newsgroups) on topics that range from welfare reform to the Simpsons. It also contains job advertisements, conference postings, sundry announcements and so forth.

- Listservs provide an avenue for professional networking, advice and help in finding resources.

Online services such as America Online, CompuServe, Prodigy offer access to extensive databases on a wide range of topics such as sports, product evaluations from *Consumer Reports*, financial information, etc.

The Internet contains live radio broadcasts including news, talk shows, etc.

Apart from news and information, the Net is a repository for thousands of freeware (free to the public) and shareware (try and buy it if you like) software programs. Technical advice, some of which comes directly from software and hardware developers, can be found online. So can software and hardware reviews, new products, patches and updates for existing software programs, stock quotes, etc.

The Net includes entertainment features like "chat rooms" (where people engage in online and real-time discussions), computer games, movies, sounds, 3D worlds, photographs, entertainment news, restaurant reviews, film and literary reviews, movie clips, automobile tests, etc.

More companies, organizations and agencies are going online daily. Virtually anything from around the globe can be found on the Internet.

GETTING STARTED: HARDWARE, SOFTWARE AND SERVICE PROVIDERS

Ways to Get on the Internet

Hardwired and remote access are the two basic ways to get on the Internet.

1. Hardwired access means that the computer you are working on is directly connected to a larger network, which is turn is connected to the Internet. This can occur in a university computing center (or an academic department hardwired into a university network), a

large corporate office, or a large governmental agency. Hardwired access to the Internet requires a terminal attached to a network or another computer.

2.	Remote access to the Internet involves phoning into a network (or another computer) using a computer and a modem. Remote access requires three basic components: (a) a computer, (b) a modem, and (c) a commercial or non-profit Internet service provider.

The Net can be accessed either through a text-based or a graphical environment. A text-based Internet environment is based on typed letters and words (pictures and icons are unavailable in this environment). The user is required to use typing commands (some of which can be arcane and difficult to learn) to access e-mail, Web pages and FTP sites. Text-based Internet access will give you the text on the WWW pages, but not the graphics. In short, you see the words but not the pictures or icons. Because many Web pages are very graphically attractive, a text-based environment misses much of the Web's popular appeal. On the other hand, if you are only interested in e-mail or Listserv discussion groups, text-based access may be all you really need.

Conversely, a graphical environmental is based on pictures and icons. By using a mouse, you enter and navigate the Internet in a pictorial or icon-based environment. E-mail, Web pages and FTP sites are accessed by using your mouse to click on a button, picture or icon. With a graphical environment you gain the intuitive value of icons which act as visual cues.

The easiest way to access the Internet is in a university computing center. You simply open an account, get a username, a password, and an e-mail address. Afterward, you just log on. In most cases, Internet access is free (often it is part of required student fees) since the hardware, software, and Internet access are provided by the university. You only need to learn the software and how to navigate the Net. Compared to using a modem for remote access, a hardwired network provides substantially faster access times to Web sites. In fact, accessing a Web site via a hardwired computer can be more than four to five times faster than using a modem.

Despite its ease, problems exist with relying on university computer centers for Internet access. First, not all computer centers offer graphical Internet access. Secondly, Internet-based research can consume untold hours of time. Occupying terminals in computer centers for several hours at a time ties up those computers for other users. (It may also be uncomfortable to sit in a small cubicle for several hours.) Thirdly, computer centers often restrict the hours students can work. Since the Internet relies on telephone lines, the slowest times tend to be the most heavily trafficked ones, generally during the day. Consequently, the Net is often fastest early in the morning, late at night, or on weekends, the times that most users will access the Net from home.

THE HARDWARE NEEDED TO REMOTELY ACCESS THE INTERNET

Remote graphical access to the Internet requires the following:

- A 386-based (or faster) personal computer (PC) with at least 8 Megabytes (MB) of Random Access Memory (RAM). While you can get graphical Internet access with a 386 or 486-based PC, the faster the computer the faster the software will run. Running graphically-based Internet software on a 386-based computer will seem impossibly slow. *An Intel 286-based or lower computer will not run the software needed to graphically access the Net.*

- A 14,400 KBPS (Kilo Bits Per Second) or faster modem. While a 14.4 KBPS is the *absolute minimum* speed for a graphical Internet connection, in reality it is too slow. The current standard is a **Cable** modem.

- A mouse with at least two clickable buttons.

- A live telephone line.

- An Internet service provider (ISP).

- Dial-up software and a Web browser.

Alternatively, you can access the Internet in a text-based environment with almost any size computer and slow modem (e.g., 9600 KBPS).

Tips on Choosing a Computer

For the first time buyer, the computer marketplace is a minefield of choices. Some of these choices are cheaper in the short-run but more expensive in the long-term. For example, some computer companies have recently marketed an "Internet computer." If this computer only has the capability to access the Internet, it is a waste of money since it will not allow you to do the other tasks (writing papers, creating charts, statistics, spreadsheets, etc.) associated with computer use.

Most newer computers use the Intel Pentium-based CPU chip (or its equivalent). If you are in the market for a new computer and you want graphical Internet access (i.e., if you plan on using Windows 95/98), we recommend at least a Pentium-level 100 MHZ (or its equivalent) PC. Graphical interface (GUI) Web browser programs such as the Netscape and MS Explorer require a minimum of 8 Megabytes (MB) of Random Access Memory (RAM). Most users find that these

Web browsers run too slowly with only 8 MB of Ram and that 16 MB is more acceptable. In fact, many computer experts believe that the most effective upgrade on a 486-based PC is to increase the random access memory (RAM) from 8 to 16 MB.

Most new software is being developed for Windows 95/98 rather than older versions of Windows (e.g., Windows 3.xx). (**Note**: Software designed solely for Windows 95/98 will not run on older versions of Windows, although most software for Windows 3.xx will run on Windows 95/98.) Windows 95/98 programs simply run faster and better on Pentium-level computers.

To properly run Web browsers and other Windows 95/98-based software computers should have at minimum:

A 75 MHZ or faster Pentium processor

A VGA graphics card with at least 1 MB of memory

8 MB of RAM (16 MB is highly recommended)

A 14" SVGA color monitor with at least a .28 dots per inch (DPI) screen

A two-button mouse

A hard drive with a minimum of 500 MB of disk storage. Both Netscape and MS Explorer take up considerable hard disk space — the full installation can consume from 20 to 60 MB. In addition, a full installation of the WordPerfect Suite version 7.0 for Windows 95 uses over 200 MB of hard drive space. Because of this, we strongly recommend that any new computer should have a hard drive with at least 1 Gigabyte or more of hard disk space.

Tips on Choosing a Modem

Choosing a modem is almost as complicated as choosing a computer. In general, there are four kinds of modems: *internal modems* that located inside a desktop PC, *external modems* that attach to the serial port, *PCMCIA modems* that fit into a PCMCIA slot in a notebook or desktop PC, and *ISDN modems* that requires the installation of a special telephone line. In general, the first three modems perform equally well.

One advantage of an external modem is that its external LED lights can help diagnose problems and indicate whether you are downloading a file or even still online. However, the dial up software included with Windows 95/98 emulates many of these functions. Secondly, external modems are easier to install since you don't have to open the case to access a free slot on the motherboard. The external modem also takes up desktop space, is a little more expensive than an internal modem, and requires an electrical outlet. The ISDN modem is four times faster than the other three. Unfortunately, it requires the installation of a separate ISDN phone line which also involves an additional telephone company charge (often high) for using the line. At this point, ISDN modems are cost-prohibitive for all but the most addicted Netaholics. Should ISDN prices come down in the future, this technology could well replace the other three types of modems.

Graphic Internet access requires at least a 14.4 KBPS modem. Optimally, the modem should operate at speeds of 33.6 KBPS or faster (56.6 KBPS is the new industry standard). A 28.8 or 33.6 KBPS modem should be V.34 and V.32 BIS compatible. In addition, any new modem should also have fax capabilities at 14.4 BPS. A modem will only operate at speeds that are supported by the phone line it is connected to. In other words, if you have a "dirty" phone line (full of static) the speed of the modem will be drastically reduced. If you are certain that your oftware is installed properly and you consistently connect at speeds significantly less than the highest speed of your modem, you should ask the telephone company to check your phone lines.

Although the new industry standard for modems is 56.6 KBPS, some clarification is necessary. First, while a 56.6 modem will theoretically receive data at 56.6 KBPS it will only transmit data at 33.6 KBPS. Secondly because of less than perfect telephone lines, most 56.6 modems will not connect at 56.6 KBPS. In fact, many users never connect beyond 46 KBPS on a 56.6 modem. Any new 56.6 KBPS should use the new V.90 industry standard or be upgradeable to that standard.

While slower modems are less expensive than faster modems, they slow down Internet connection times, especially when it involves heavy graphics. Slower modems increase online time which can increase user charges. In the long-run, a slower modem may end up costing you more rather than less. It is also a good idea to purchase a modem surge protector to protect against phone line surges. For text-based Internet access a slower 9600 BPS modem is sufficient.

CHOOSING A SERVICE PROVIDER

You must enter the Internet through a host computer connected to the Net. As noted earlier, remote Internet access may be provided free by your university. Alternatively, you can gain free access to the Net by going through a Freenet organization. These organizations are staffed by volunteers and often do not provide graphical Web access. Information on a Freenet organization in your area is found by contacting the National Public Telecomputing Network (NPTN), 30680 Bainbridge Rd., Solon Springs, OH; (216) 498-4050 (**http://www.nptn.org**). If your university does not provide free Internet access (or you choose not to go with a Freenet provider), you will have to shop around for the best Internet service provider at the lowest possible cost.

The number of companies offering Internet access has grown dramatically over the past several years. Overall, there are two different types of Internet service providers: large online services and basic Internet providers. Large online service providers include such companies as CompuServe, **Earthlink,** America Online, Prodigy, Genie, and Delphi among others. While most of these companies offer basic Internet service, they also offer also extra features like large and specialized databases, chat rooms, discussion groups, technical forums, access to stock quotes, newspapers, magazines, etc. Some companies charge extra for additional or premium services. In contrast, the basic Internet service provider only furnishes Internet access. These companies offer no special services beyond what is already on the Net. In effect, they provide "plain vanilla" Internet access.

Internet-only service providers fall into two categories: large national service providers (e.g., AT&T, **Worldcom**, Sprint, IDT, etc.) and local small providers. Local Internet providers can be found by contacting computer user groups and computer clubs, browsing local computer publications, and searching through the Yellow Pages. A Web site called The List (**http://www.thelist.com**) can help you find Internet access providers in your area. Billing for Internet service is done either by adding the service cost directly to your phone bill or by having it deducted monthly from your credit card.

The costs of Internet service can differ radically between companies. Some companies charge a modest monthly rate for a fixed number of online hours (usually 10-20 hours a month), after which they charge by the hour. Alternatively, some large ISPs have a fixed-rate charge with an unlimited number of online hours. The decision to use a large online provider or a "plain vanilla" one depends upon your needs. If you are only interested in doing limited research, entering discussion groups, joining Listservs and sending e-mail, a less expensive Internet access provider may be sufficient. On the other hand, you may want the services and databases that only large online service providers like CompuServe, Prodigy and America Online provide.

Choosing a cost-effective ISP can be confusing. Many ISPs offer plans which appear inexpensive but can turn out to be very costly in the long-run.

The following is a brief guide to help you choose an ISP:

- Does the ISP offer graphical Internet access? For graphical Internet access the ISP must use modems with speeds of 28.8 BPS (or higher). Your modem will only connect at the fastest speed of the modem at the other end. If the host modem is slower than 28.8 BPS, your faster modem will drop down to that speed. On the other hand, if your modem is only 14.4 KBPS and the host modem is 28.8 KBPS, the host will slow down to accommodate your modem.

- What is the hourly versus the unlimited Internet access rate? Try to anticipate the amount of time you will spend on the Net each month to judge the best deal. If you plan on spending a lot of time on the Net, a flat unlimited rate is the best option. Shop around if the ISP does not offer a flat rate for unlimited (or a high number of hours) Internet access.

- Does the ISP offer e-mail? Without e-mail capabilities, an ISP is too limited. Does the ISP charge for sending or receiving e-mail? If so, you might want to shop around for a flat rate that includes e-mail.

- Is there a set-up fee? Some ISPs charge a one-time set-up fee. Since set-up fees can be costly, shopping around will save money.

- Does the ISP offer free software? If software is provided, what kind is it? Is it proprietary or industry-standard software like Netscape or Microsoft's Internet Explorer? Proprietary software may be too limited to access the newest features of the Net. Moreover, providing software is not especially important since Web browsers like Netscape and Microsoft are free to everyone. In addition, dial-up software is a standard feature of Windows 9598.

- What kind of technical support does the ISP offer? Is it free? What are the technical support hours? Is technical support a toll call or an 800 or local phone number? Before signing up, you may want to call technical support just to see how long the wait is and whether you can get through to a live person.

- Are the ISPs Internet access lines frequently busy? You may want to get the ISPs access phone number to determine whether you will be able to get through at the desired times.

If you choose an hourly rate ISP, there are ways to cut down your online time. For one, you can compose your e-mail letters offline. This can be done by writing a letter in your word processor and then cutting and pasting it into your e-mail program. When you are done, simply phone the ISP to send the message. Secondly, you can explore "touch and go" and "flash essions" that let you go online to check your mail and then immediately log off. When you have written your messages and want to post them, the program will then log you back on.

DIALING INTO THE INTERNET

If you are using a basic ISP or your university's remote Internet access line, you may need the following information in order to set up your software and get online:

4. A *login name*. The login name is frequently the same as the letters to the left of @ in your e-mail address. You can often choose your own login name; many users opt to use their first initial and last names. For example, HJohnson. Login names are best kept simple to make it easy for you and others to remember your e-mail address.

5. A *login password*. You can usually choose your login password or change the one that is assigned to you. Passwords should be easy to remember and can be made up of either numbers or letters. To ensure a higher level of security, many computer experts warn against using your Social Security number or birth date since these are relatively easy for hackers to find.

6. An *e-mail* address. E-mail addresses are usually your login name plus the address of your server. For example, HJohnson@zd.edu

7. A *pop account* is the address that your **incoming** e-mail will be sent to, which is not the same as your actual e-mail address. This can look something like post-office.zd.edu. It can also look like dsmith@post-office.zd.edu.

8. *SMTP* is the servers address for routing your **outgoing** e-mail. In effect, incoming and outgoing mail use two different paths on the server. In fact, you can check your e-mail on

one server or ISP and send out your e-mail from another server or ISP. A typical SMTP address might look like smtp.zd.edu or mailhost.att.net.

9.   The *News Server* address. This is the address you access for finding and downloading USENET newsgroups. A typical news server address might look like news.zd.edu or news1.att.net.

7.   The *Domain Name Server* (DNS) is the Internet address of your server. Some servers have primary and secondary DNS addresses. A primary or secondary DNS might look like 127.230.151.3

8.   The phone number(s) to call to access the Internet. There may be separate numbers for 14.4, 28.8 and 56.6 KBPS phone lines.

9.   The phone number and hours for technical support.

10. The address of the ISPs WWW home page. This page will often contain important information.

Dial-Up Software

Remote Internet access requires dial-up software to form a bridge between your PC and the computer or network you are calling into. Specifically, this software dials up the remote site and establishes the connection and protocol for the Internet session. Once connected, you enter your username and password.

Almost any kind of DOS or Windows dial-up software that emulates a computer terminal is sufficient in a text-based environment. This includes the terminal software included with

Windows 3.xx or DOS-based programs like Procomm (commercial and shareware versions) and Telix (shareware), to name a few. **(Text based access is now obsolete)**

There are three forms for distributing software: (1) commercial software sold in stores or online, (2) shareware that is distributed on a "try and buy if you like" basis, and (3) freeware (free software). Distributed online, shareware is often time-limited (e.g., it expires on a certain date and either stops working or begins displaying annoying "nag screens"). Shareware may also contain permanent "nag screens" or have inoperable features. While sometimes quite good, shareware may not be as stable or comprehensive as commercial software. Freeware is also distributed online and provided without cost (occasionally voluntary contributions are asked). This kind of software is sometimes developed under a government grant, or by a company that offers a "light" rather than a full-featured version of its commercial software. Both shareware and freeware are often distributed by computer user groups.

Software choices are more limited if you want to remotely access the Internet in a graphical environment. First, you must run Microsoft Windows (Windows 95/98) or another graphical operating system like IBM's OS2. Secondly, your dial-up software must employ a specific protocol. If you are using Windows 3.xx, this will require an additional dial-up software program like TCP Manager, a shareware program found at: **http://www.trumpet.com.au**. On the other hand, if you are using Windows 95/98 the dial-up software is included in the program. Some dial-up software programs like TCP Manager and Windows 95/98 allow you to save your username and password thereby eliminating the inconvenience of retyping these each time you connect.

Choosing a dial-up software program is important because it partly determines the stability of your connection to the remote site. If you are using a Pentium-based PC and Windows 95/98, you should run only 32-bit communication programs. Running the 32-bit versions of Netscape or MS Explorer requires a 32-bit dial-up software program like the one included with Windows 95/98. However, setting up the dial-up program for Windows 95/98 can be complicated. To ease matters, you may want to consult a technically-inclined friend or ask your Internet provider to walk you through the process.

A 16-bit dial-up program like TCP Manager will work under the Windows 95/98 32-bit operating system. However, a 32-bit dial-up program will *not* work under Windows 3.1x (a 16-bit operating system). Moreover, the 32-bit versions of MS Explorer and Netscape are designed for Windows 95/98 and will *not* work under a 16-bit dial-up program. So, if you are using TCP Manager as your dial-up program in Windows 95/98, you *must* download and use only the 16-bit versions of MS Internet Explorer and Netscape even though you are operating in a 32-bit environment. In short, for the 32-bit versions of these web browsers to work, you *must* be connected online via a 32-bit dial-up program like the one included with Windows 95/98.

INTERNET CONVENTIONS

Before examining the various parts of the Net, it is first important to examine Internet-related protocols. First, capital letters are rarely used when typing e-mail addresses since non-capitalized addresses are easier to read. However, the first letter or two in an e-mail address may be capitalized to make it stand out (e.g., HJones@zd.edu). Secondly, e-mail letters typed totally in capitalized letters are considered bad protocol — the words "scream" at the reader. Using only ower caps for proper names, e.g., president clinton, is also considered inappropriate. Thirdly, the word "Dear" is rarely used since e-mail tends to be a less formal medium than business letters. Fourthly, the term "at" in an e-mail address is written as @. A period (.) Is referred to as a dot. So, Djones-at-zd.edu is written as Djones@zd.edu. There are no blank spaces in either e-mail or WWW addresses. However, there can be a lower dash (which often substitutes for a space). For example, an e-mail address can read D_jones@zd.edu.

Internet and e-mail addresses can contain important information about the location and type of site you are visiting. For example, the last two or three letters in an address can help identify important characteristics of the site:

.edu is an educational institution

. com is a commercial company or a commercial Internet provider

.org is a non-profit organization

.gov refers to a governmental agency or office

.net is an Internet provider or a network

.bit is BITNET

With the exception of the United States, all Internet and e-mail addresses have a country code which is the last two letters of the address. For example,

.ar is Argentina

.au is Australia

.ca is Canada

.de is Germany

.eg is Egypt

.fr is France

.il is Israel

.jp is Japan

.mx is Mexico

.no is Norway

.uk is United Kingdom

.za is South Africa

The Internet has begun to develop its own colloquialisms, Among other terms, "FYI" means "for your information," "BTW" means "by the way" and FAQ (a common acronym in Net language) means "frequently asked questions."

SURFING THE INTERNET WITH YOUR WEB BROWSER

The World Wide Web (WWW) is a graphical, easy-to-navigate interface for viewing documents or graphics on the Internet. These documents, as well as the links between them, comprise a "web" of information. In effect, the Web is like a big library. Web sites are similar to books in the library and Web pages are like specific pages in those books. A collection of Web pages is known as a Web site. To graphically access Web sites you need a program called a Web browser, which lets you navigate the Net, access WWW pages and download and copy information, files, and programs. Web browsers like Netscape and MS Explorer (through its add-ons) also include the ability to read and send e-mail messages and to engage in newsgroup activities.

Your journey through the Web begins from a Web page known as a homepage, which is similar to the cover page or the Table of Contents of a book. By default, most Web browsers automatically log you onto their homepage. However, Web browsers also allow you to start from *any* Web page on the Net. Apart from functioning like a compass for the Net, homepages are important since they are frequently updated with important information. So, if you are a student at the University of Houston-GSSW and regularly want to find out what is happening on campus, you might choose the University of Houston-GSSW's Web site as your homepage. Every time you log on you will arrive first at the University of Houston-GSSW, where you can check the activities calendar or other information.

The WWW is a network of sources for information and entertainment. The predecessor of the WWW was Gopher, which organized information into simple text documents and menus. While Gopher was an important part of the Internet's history, it lacked the true hypertext and graphical capabilities which make the WWW so successful. WAIS was another early part of the Internet, and was used by institutions to search and index large amounts of data. Both Gopher and WAIS are still used today and can be accessed directly by Netscape and the MS Internet Explorer. The address for Gopher sites is written as: gopher://gopher......

While the WWW contains news, images, documents, computer and data analysis programs, newspapers, magazines, governmental and non-governmental data and records, stock quotes, and job opportunities, it also includes entertainment features like computer games, movies, sounds, 3D worlds, entertainment news, restaurant reviews, film and literary reviews, movie clips, etc. These sites are scattered around the world. (One of the advantages of the

Internet is that you can navigate the globe on the price of a local call.) By using a Web browser like Netscape or MS Explorer, you can visit various Web sites and download data, programs, and graphics; copy Web pages (or parts of them); and in some cases, e-mail the person(s) who set up the Web page.

Hypertext makes the Web easier to navigate. In fact, they are the connecting strands that form the WWW. Using a file format called HTML (hypertext markup language), hypertext are embedded commands in Web pages that let you jump (hyperlink) from one Web page to another. "Surfing the Web" simply means following embedded hyperlinks, which usually take the form of buttons, underlined or blinking text or highlighted graphics. When the mouse cursor is moved to an active image or highlighted text a small hand appears letting you know that it is a hyperlink. Clicking on the left mouse button leads you to a related Web page, subject, or document. Hyperlinks can lead to pages that contain movies, pictures, or sounds. Because most Web pages use graphics extensively, they are often attractive, and in some cases, even artistic.

Each Internet site has a unique address called a URL (Uniform Resource Locator), which is similar to a postal address or a telephone number in that it lets you locate a site on the Net. You can give a URL to someone anywhere in the world and they will be able to access the same Internet site. To access a Web site through Netscape or MS Explorer, you enter a URL address, which often (but not always) begins with http://www. . . .

Web Browsers

Although several Web browsers are currently available, the two most popular are Netscape and MS Internet Explorer. Both are sophisticated Web browsers that allow for "plug-in" software (i.e., software that enhances Internet functions by playing radio programs, accessing virtual reality and 3D sites, making long distance calls through the Internet, etc.). Both are also free. Netscape can be downloaded from **http://www.netscape.com** and Microsoft's Internet Explorer from **http://www.microsoft.com.**

Netscape and MS Explorer have similar interfaces because they do the same things. The following explains some of the components of Netscape 3.03 (see Figure 2). Although the buttons on MS Explorer 5.01 have slightly different names, the program has similar components (see Figure 1).

Figure 1. Microsoft Internet Explorer Ver. 5.01

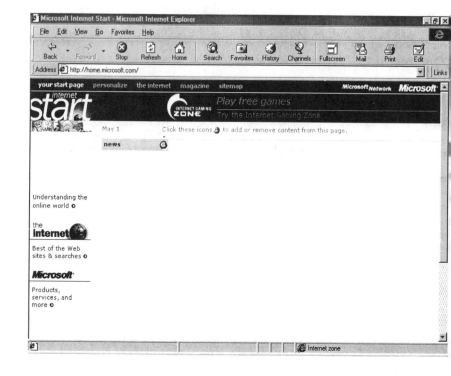

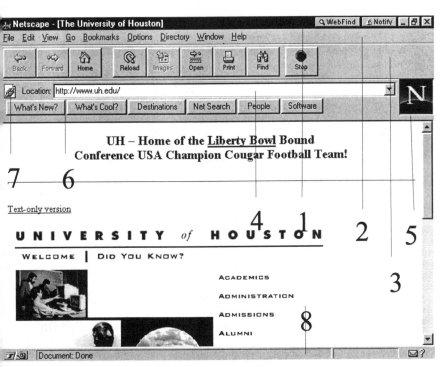

Figure 2. Netscape Ver. 4.0

No. 1: The uppermost top line is where the name of the Web page being visited appears. In this example, we are visiting the home page of the University of Houston.

No. 2: Referred to as the menu bar, this line houses the various functions of the program including bookmarks, and under options, it contains fields for setting preferences and configuring the program.

No. 3: This line contains eight boxes. From right to left: (1) the *Stop* button stops the current load action (useful if a site is slow and you run out of patience waiting for the graphics to load), (2) the *Find* button finds specific text on a Web page (useful if you are in a long document and want to find a string of text or see whether key words are on a Web page), (3) the *Print* button prints the Web page you are on, (4) the *Open* button opens a networked document, (5) the *Images* button loads images in the message, (6) the *Reload* button reloads a web page in the event that the transmission was halted, (7) the *Home* button brings you automatically to your default home page, (8) the *Forward* button brings you forward to the next page in the history list (you can only access this button if you have gone backward to a previously viewed web page), and (9) the *Back* button moves you backward to a previously read web page.

No. 4: This is the location box. It shows the URL that you are visiting. It is also the place where you type in the address of a web site you want to visit. to. Clicking the down arrow on the right side of the box brings up a list of the last 15 web sites you have visited.

No. 5: This is the Netscape icon. Double-clicking this icon will take you directly to Netscape's home page.

o. 6: These six buttons function as shortcuts. Starting from right to left: (1) the *Software* button takes you to a Netscape page where you can download the newest version of the program, (2) the *People* button takes you to an Internet "white pages" where you can look up a name and locate someone's e-mail address, (3) the *Net Search* button takes you to rotating Internet search engines where you can search for a name or a specific topic, (4) the *Destinations* button takes you to sites that use advanced Netscape technology, (5) the *What's Cool* takes you to sites that Netscape thinks are interesting, and (6) the *What's New* button takes you to the other sites that Netscape staff think are worthwhile.

o. 7: If this small icon is double-clicked the address of the web site on the line is saved to the Windows clipboard.

o. 8: The bottom status line in Netscape shows potentially important information. A broken key in the left-hand corner means that the site you are viewing has no security. If you are not using your credit card on this site or filling out an important form the lack of security is generally not a problem. In a secure site, you will see a solid blue line at the top of the screen and an unbroken key on the bottom left-hand side. The status line tells you how much of the Web page has been loaded. If the site developer knows Java script, a message may roll across this bar like a ticker-tape. The envelope icon on the far right-hand side loads Netscape's e-mail program. A question mark means that Netscape hasn't checked your e-mail during the session that you are logged on. Netscape can be configured to check your e-mail at pre-arranged intervals, and when you receive mail, the number of letters you receive will replace the question mark.

Tips for Browsing the Web

The WWW can be excruciatingly slow during peak traffic periods. This slowdown is exacerbated by loading graphics during peak traffic periods which further slow the transmission. One way to shorten access times is to view Web pages without graphics. This can be done in two ways. First, many Web sites offer an option to view their page in a text-only (minus graphics) mode. Alternatively, you can turn off the auto-loading of images in your Web browser. In Netscape, go to the *Options* menu and turn off *Auto Loading Images*. In MS Explorer go to the Options menu and uncheck the *Show Pictures*, *Play Sounds* and the *Play Video* boxes.

It is tedious to retype the same address each time you access a Web site. It is also frustrating to lose or forget the address of an interesting site that you accidentally found while surfing the Net. Interesting and frequently used Web sites or search engines can be permanently added to a "Bookmarks" file in Netscape or a "Favorites" file in MS Explorer. Once these Web pages are added as bookmarks, they are permanently saved. Bookmarks can be rearranged and organized into categories representing different kinds of sites. In Netscape you save a Web site by clicking on *Bookmarks* in the main menu and then clicking on *Add Bookmark* (see Figure 3). In Internet Explorer, click on *Favorites* and then *Add to Favorites*. One word of caution: carefully organized and categorized bookmark files can contain several hundred or even several thousand Web sites. It takes a great deal of time to find these sites and then organize them topically. Bookmark files should be backed up on a diskette or tape drive in the same way as data files. Hard disk drives will always fail. It is only a question of time when that will happen.

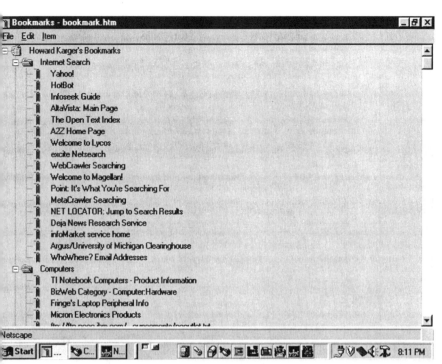

Figure 3. Netscape Ver. 4 Bookmark File

SEARCHING THE NET FOR INFORMATION

Searching for information is one of the most important yet time-consuming tasks in Internet research. One reason for this is that the Internet is a large virtual library, one that contains tens of many millions of documents and Web sites.

Locating information on the Internet is similar to finding information in a normal library. You enter the library knowing what you want and then search for the information. For example, if you want to find information on the Family Medical Leave Act (FMLA) signed into law in 1993, you would go into your university library and look it up either through a card catalog or by an online subject search. You would then proceed to the stacks containing the relevant books and articles. Once there, you might decide to narrow your search to the latest interpretation of the FMLA. After finding the information you need, you either check it out or photocopy it. What you did was to simply narrow your subject search, find the information, and take away what you needed. An Internet search operates in the same way. The following represents the steps in a typical Internet search.

Choosing a Search Engine

Several companies and/or organizations offer search engines which compile and organize the multitude of documents and information found on the Internet. The information is then categorized under key words and subject headings. In effect, this creates a huge subject card index that functions in the same way as an online subject search in a normal library. The only difference is that the scope of the Internet search is usually broader than a typical library search. Search engines are usually free, since companies make money by posting advertisements on their sites. Most Web browsers such as Netscape and Explorer have built-in hyperlinks to search engines.

There are basically two kinds of search engines: (1) search engines that function as directories which sort millions of documents into categories such as entertainment, recreation, health, news, sports, etc., and (2) search engines that function as indexes that analyze the full text of millions of Internet documents and rank them by the number of times a key word(s) appears. Directory-based search engines are normally used for general searches (e.g., auto racing), while more specialized searches (e.g., an analysis of Americorps) require an index-based search engine. These generalities do not always hold and you should feel free to experiment with a range of search engines.

The choice of a search engine is an individual preference. All search engines have a slightly different look and feel. In addition, some search engines are better at finding information in certain topic areas than others. If one search engine does not yield satisfactory results, you should run the same query on another engine. Although Netscape and MS Explorer have built-in links to various search engines, it may take longer to go through their networks than to access a search engine directly. These Web browsers may also not have hyperlinks to the wide variety of search engines available. The following list includes some of the larger search engines:

Sites with Links to Search Engines

   http://nln.com (Net Locator is a good link to major search engines)

   http://www.search.com (C/Net hyperlinks to dozens of search engines)

Search Engines

http://www.google.com

http://www.yahoo.com (Yahoo is the best-known directory-based search engine)

http://www.hotbot.com (Hotbot is a good index-based search engine)

http://altavista.com (AltaVista is one of the oldest index-based search engines)

http://www.lycos.com (Lycos is a directory-based search engine)

http://www.excite.com (Excite is a popular index-based search engine)

http://www.pointcom.com (The Point is a directory-based search engine)

http://www.magellan.excite.com (Magellan is an index-based search engine)

http://www.go.com (GO is a large directory-based search engine)

http://www.webcrawler.com (Web Crawler is a directory-based search engine)

http://archie.emnet.co.uk/   (Archieplex is a good Archie search engine)

More specialized search sites include:

http://www.deja.com (Deja News finds information only in newsgroups)

http://www.whowhere.lycos.com (Who? Where? is a "White Pages" of Internet users)

Limiting the Parameters of a Net Search

Without establishing some parameters for an Internet search, you will find yourself overwhelmed by the sheer number of information sources available. As an example, if you devoted 10 hours a day to studying the Internet, and spent one minute on each Web page, it would take over 5 years to explore the million plus Web pages currently on the Internet. This does not include the several thousand new Web pages being added monthly.

You can limit a Web search by choosing key words or phrases. For example, using the above illustration, you might type in the words "FMLA" or "Family Medical Leave Act." But, by using "FMLA" you could end up with hundreds of sources that would be time-consuming to sort through. So, you can decide to limit your search by using key words (rather than a single word). In this instance, you could type in "Interpretations of the FMLA," which would bring up fewer sources.

Most search engines arrange the list of "hits" in terms of relevance. In other words, how closely the word(s) you chose match the word(s) found on the Web page. Choosing from the most promising "hits," click on the hyperlink (usually underlined and in blue text) and you will jump to the source. You can then go back to the search engine's original list (or go backward to any other previously viewed page) by clicking the *Back* button on your Web browser. Conversely, you can move forward again by clicking on the *Forward* button. If the site you are trying to reach is busy or not responding, hit the *Stop* button and choose another source from the list.

Search Conventions

There are several conventions in an Internet search. First, you must click in the search box and type either a word, a few words, or a phrase that describes what you want to find. While you can use words and phrases without special symbols or punctuation, at other times you may want to refine your search by using special syntaxes like capitalizing proper names such as "December" and "California." If you capitalize adjacent names, some search engines may treat the words as a single name. If you don't capitalize a proper name, it may be treated like any other word. In addition, you can type a name with an identifier after it (e.g., Buckminster Fuller, architect).

When you search for several names or topics, use commas to separate them. For example, to search for Bill Clinton and the Presidency, type: "Bill Clinton, Presidency". Omitting the comma between proper names causes them to be treated as one single long name. A search for Bill Clinton Presidency may not yield good results.

You can use double quotation marks (" ") or hyphens (-) between words that are part of a phrase. You can also use double quotation marks around words that must appear next to each other. For example, to find pages that describe the federal budget deficit, type: "federal budget deficit". Without the double quotation marks, some search engines would find sites that include the word "federal," sites that include the word "budget," and sites that include the word "deficit." You can also use hyphens between words that must appear within one word of each other, e.g., to search for information about budget deficits, type: budget-deficits.

You can also put a plus sign (+) in front of words that must be contained in documents found in the search. For example, to find out about health care in Houston, type: health care +Houston. (Do not put a space between the plus sign and the word.) Conversely, you can put a minus sign (-) in front of words that should not appear in any documents found by the search. For example, to find all resources that contain health care but not cost, type: health care -cost. For the widest search, choose "The World Wide Web" when asked for the location of the search.

VIRUSES ON THE NET

It is important to separate hyperbole from fact when it comes to computer viruses. Your computer cannot catch a virus by simply clicking on a Web site, even if it displays graphics and plays movies, sound or 3D files. (You can, however, experience damage if you encounter a malicious Java or Active X applet.) Nothing "automatic" within the browser can cause a virus to get into your computer. You can catch a virus if you run a program or application that you downloaded from the Internet. Any program that you download from the Net or get from a friend should be checked for viruses before you run it. New breeds of viruses can do extensive damage to software, data files and hardware.

New viruses are being created daily and anti-virus software programs are continually being upgraded to stop or eliminate them. Most anti-virus programs operate on three levels. First, they have a component that protects the computer from contacting a virus; the second component scans the computers memory and its hard disk and floppy disk drives to see if a virus is present; and the third component tries to clean a virus. Any anti-virus program you buy should have all three components. Moreover, it is necessary is to find an anti-virus program that is updated regularly (e.g., Norton Anti-Virus, McAfee's VirusScan, Dr. Solomon's, Thunderbyte Anti-Virus, etc.). Many of these programs can be downloaded directly from the Internet:

VirusScan: **http://www.mcafeeb2b.com/**

Norton Anti-Virus: **http://www.symantec.com**

Dr. Solomon's Anti-Virus: **http://www.drsolomon.com**

Thunderbyte Anti-Virus: **http://www.norman.com/tbav.shtml**

IBM Anti-Virus: **http://www.ibm.com**

E-MAIL

E-mail is fast becoming the communications avenue of choice for many human service professionals. Due to its inexpensiveness, speed, and ease of use, it is quickly evolving into a substitute for telephone, fax, and postal communications. E-mail letters and memos are typed directly into the computer and sent over telephone lines via the Internet. In most cases, local, national and foreign recipients usually receive the letter within hours (usually minutes) after it is sent. Although e-mail letters are generally free, some ISPs charge for e-mail access.

To use e-mail you must first open an account with your university or ISP. You will then need a username, a password (your e-mail password is often different than your login password), and an e-mail address. Once online, most letters and memos are composed of the following: (1) the e-mail address of the recipient, (2) your e-mail address (usually added automatically by your e-mail program), (3) a title or subject heading identifying the message, (4) the main body of the letter, and (5) your optional electronic "signature" (e.g., your phone, physical address, e-mail address, fax number, etc.).

Apart from handling simple letters and memos, most e-mail programs can also send attachments (e.g., documents, photographs or even software programs) as separate files. This is a useful function if you are writing an article or professional paper and want to keep the formatting intact. By sending the file as an attachment the recipient receives the document exactly the way you composed it.

If you send an attachment, make sure that the message is encoded in the same format used by the recipient. (You can ask what encoding format they have configured their e-mail program to use.) Alternatively, in a Windows environment you can cut, paste and insert information from a word processing program directly into an e-mail letter. Unlike sending an attachment, the recipient receives the e-mail as a letter not a separate file. Cutting and pasting an e-mail letter into a word processing program requires extensive reformatting (e.g., it may have hard returns at the end of each line) if the receiver wants to use it as a separate and "clean" document.

You can also send the same e-mail letter to a few people or to large groups. To do this, find the line in the e-mail program that says "cc:" and list the addresses of the recipients you want to receive the letter. You can also save typing strokes by setting up a nicknames file in your e-mail program. For example, if you have a friend named Don, go to the nicknames menu of your e-mail program and type in the full e-mail address of the recipient. When writing a letter type in "Don" on the line that says "to" or "recipient" and send the letter.

Most e-mail programs allow you to put in a "signature" — e.g., your e-mail address, title, physical address, telephone or fax number. This is useful if people want to contact you later in ways other than e-mail. You can determine which information you want to be included in a signature file and how that information will look.

There are two ways to respond to an e-mail message. First, you can send an entirely new message. Alternatively, you can reply to a message by quoting all or part of it. In the latter, highlight the letter you want to respond to and click on *Reply.* The original e-mail message will have a ">" next to each line. Scroll down to the parts you want to answer and type in a response.

Or, you can delete the entire contents of the old message and type in a new one. Replying to an existing message is often easier than writing a new one since you don't have to type in the address of the recipient.

To find the e-mail address of a sender, look at the *From:* line in the e-mail message you received. You can also use various e-mail address locator services. In addition, a directory called *People on the Web* can be found in the directory section of Internet Explorer. In Netscape, go to *Directory* on the top menu bar and then scroll down to *Internet White Pages*.

While Netscape and MS Explorer have e-mail capabilities, some users prefer separate e-mail programs. Two good graphical e-mail programs are Eudora (**http://www.qualcomm.com**) (see Figure 4) and Pegasus Mail which can be found at (**http://www.jumbo.com**). Eudora comes in two versions: Eudora Pro (commercial version) and Eudora Lite (freeware). Both Eudora and Pegasus Mail come in 16 and 32-bit versions and have a multitude of features.

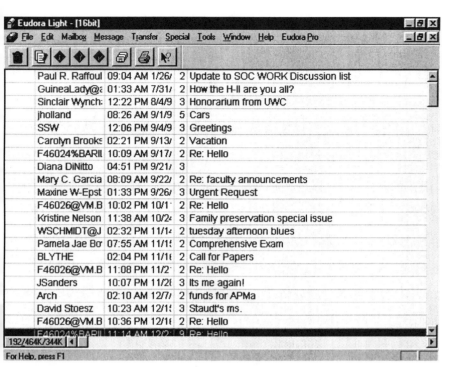

Figure 4. Eudora Lite

USENET NEWSGROUPS

Newsgroups are electronic discussion groups that let you share information and opinions with people from around the world. Most newsgroups can be accessed by anyone browsing the Net. In each newsgroup there are numerous postings (which may include graphic images or sounds) on a given subject. Usenet newsgroups allow you to reply to posted articles and to publish ("post") your own articles for others to read. Newsgroups are organized and grouped by titles using compound names such as rec.sport.basketball.college. Here, "rec" refers to recreational topics, "sport" specifies a subgroup of recreation, and so on. Newsreader software like Winvn or Free Agent (both can be downloaded from the Web) and Web browsers like Netscape and MS Explorer let you access more than 30,000 newsgroups now online. These software programs let you download posted articles and decode the pictures or graphic images found in many newsgroups.

Although Netscape and MS Explorer allow you to access and reply to newsgroups, some users prefer separate newsreader programs. While many excellent newsreaders are available, two of the more popular are Winvn (**http://www.ksc.nasa.gov/software/winvn/winvn.html**) (see Figure 5), and News Xpress (can be found in **http://www.shareware.com**). Both are free for noncommercial users.

Figure 5.

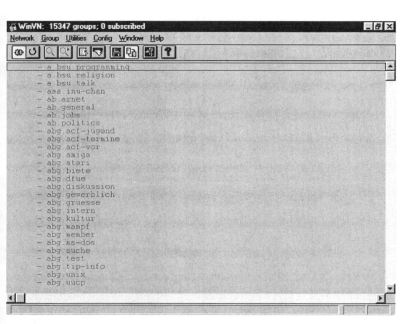

LISTSERVS

Like newsgroups, Listservs are electronic discussion groups for people with similar interests. However, unlike newsgroups participation in a Listserv does not require special software since messages are sent through e-mail. In newsgroups you retrieve messages from the news server; in Listservs messages are sent directly to you through e-mail.

Subscribing to a Listserv is usually free and subscribers can post messages (or replies to messages) that are received as e-mail by all other subscribers. Subscribers to Listservs can be active contributors or spectators that read (but don't reply to) posted messages. There is one main Listserv for social work (socwork@uafsysb.uark.edu), along with several that specialize in sub-areas (e.g., feminist social work—listproc@moose.uvm.edu). In addition, subscribing to one Listserv exposes you to the existence of other lists. In general, Listservs protect the privacy of their subscribers. Some lists are "open" (i.e., anyone on the list can send a message to the whole list), while others are "closed" (only certain people can post messages).

To subscribe to a Listserv you must send an e-mail message to the server that manages the list. (If you are using Netscape you can click on the highlighted Listserv address to e-mail a subscription.) For example, to subscribe to the social work Listserv (some Listservs use different protocols for subscribing) you would do the following:

1.   Send an e-mail message to: listserv@uafsysb.uark.edu (Leave the title or subject heading line blank)

2.   In the body of the message type: subscribe socwork [your first-name Your last-name]

3.   Send the message.

. Sometimes you will receive confirmation of your subscription and the netiquette for that Listserv group.

. Once subscribed, you send messages to: socwork@uafsysb.uark.edu.

. To unsubscribe from a Listserv follow the above steps, but instead of typing "subscribe," substitute "unsubscribe."

Caveat: While joining Listservs can be an enriching professional experience, it can also generate a lot of mail. Joining too many Listservs (or even one very active one) may result in dozens of e-mail letters a day. (The Listserv we joined generated 75 e-mail letters in one day alone.) Use prudence in deciding which and how many Listservs you will join. In addition, if you go on a long vacation, unsubscribe from Listservs before you leave. One colleague returned from a summer vacation to find 450 e-mail messages waiting for him.

A list of discussion groups of interest to social workers can be found at:

http://www.colostate.edu/Depts/SocWork/lists.html. Some social work-related discussion groups include:

socwork: Social Work
listserv@uafsysb.uark.edu
subscribe socwork [first-name] [lastname]

femsw-1: Feminist Social Work
listproc@moose.uvm.edu
subscribe femsw-1 [first-name] [lastname]

hiv-aids-psycho-social
listserv@netcom.com
subscribe hiv-aids-psycho-social

abuse-1: Child Abuse
listserv@ubvm.cc.buffalo.edu

subscribe abuse-l [first-name] [lastname]
child-maltreatment-research-l: Child Abuse Research
listproc@cornell.edu
subscribe child-maltreatment-research-l [first-name] [lastname]

ejintvio: Intimate Violence
listserv@uriacc.uri.edu
subscribe ejintvio [first-name] [lastname]

intvio-l: Intimate Violence
listserv@uriacc.uri.edu
subscribe intvio-l [first-name] [lastname]

evalten: Evaluation and Statistics
listserv@sjuvm.stjohns.edu
subscribe evalten [first-name] [lastname]

methods: Social Science Research Methods Instructors
listserv@unmvma.unm.edu
subscribe methods [first-name] [lastname]

femisa: Feminism
listproc@csf.colorado.edu
subscribe femisa [first-name] [lastname]

healthre: Healthcare Reform
listserv@ukcc.uky.edu
subscribe healthre [first-name] [lastname]

cjust-l: Criminal Justice
listserv@cunyvm.cuny.edu
subscribe cjust-l [first-name] [lastname]

cti-soc-work-uk: Computers in Social Work Education
mailbase@mailbase.ac.uk
join cti-soc-work-uk [first-name] [lastname]

computers-in-mental health
listserv@netcom.com
subscribe computers-in-mental-health

cussnet-list: Computer Use in Social Services

listserv@stat.com
subscribe cussnet [first-name] [lastname]
cwkgroup: Issues Regarding the Computerization of Behavioral,
Health, and Human Service Records
cwkgroup-request@umassd.edu
subscribe cwkgroup [first-name] [lastname]

husita-l: Human Services Information Technology Association
listserv@cornell.edu
subscribe husita-l [first-name] [lastname]

eap: Employee Assistance Programmes
majordomo@utopia.pinsight.com
subscribe eap

homeless: Homelessness
listproc@csf.colorado.edu
subscribe homeless [first-name] [lastname]

intsocwork: International Social Work
listserv@nisw.org.uk
subscribe intsocwork [first-name] [lastname]

INTERNET POLICY SITES

Several *caveats* are necessary before launching into the following list of social policy-related

Web sites. First, the number of Web sites is exploding daily. There are currently around 2 million

Web sites with several thousand being added monthly. Any list of Web sites will be incomplete

almost from the moment it is compiled. Secondly, the following list is meant only as an

introductory guide to Web sites. Part of the fun of Web surfing is following links to interesting

sites. Thirdly, this list focuses primarily on social policy-oriented sites — where possible, we

have tried to link these sites with the content and chapters in *American Social Welfare Policy*.

Fourthly, the categories we constructed will necessarily overlap. Because of an economy of

space, we have tried not to list the same Web site in more than one category. While many organizations have multiple aims and purposes, we have tried to find their central purpose in order to place them in the most appropriate category. As a result, we have undoubtedly made some mistakes, for which we apologize beforehand. Because of the sheer number of organizations with a Web presence, we have no doubt left out some important ones. For this we also apologize. Lastly, a web site is virtual — it only exists only as a small amount of hard drive space on someone's computer or network server. Web sites are often fluid since many organizations and individuals rent or borrow space on a network server. As a result, some of the Web sites listed below may no longer be in operation (or they may have moved) by the time this supplement is published. Given these warnings, happy surfing!

A Partial Listing of Policy-Oriented Web Sites

Aging

Welcome to AARP's WebPlace: http://www.aarp.org/
Administration on Aging: http://www.aoa.dhhs.gov/
The Gerontological Society of America: http://www.geron.org/
GeroWeb: http://www.iog.wayne.edu/geroweb.html
Directory of WEB and Gopher Aging Sites: Main Menu:
    http://www.AoA.DHHS.GOV/aoa/webres/craig.htm
Aging & Dementia Web Resources: http://www.biostat.wustl.edu/ALZHEIMER/submit.html
Senior I-Net Home Page: http://www.senior-inet.com/
AAHSA: http://www.senior.com/aahsa/**(AAHSA not found)**
SeniorNet: http://www.seniornet.com/
ElderCare Information Network, Inc.: http://www.eldercare.com
SPRY Home Page: http://www.spry.org/
AFAR Home Page: http://www.afar.org/
Huffington Center on Aging: http://www.hcoa.org
Duke U. Center for Aging: http://www.geri.duke.edu/
WSU Institute of Gerontology: http://www.iog.wayne.edu/
Caregiver Survival Resources: http://www.caregiver911.com
SIUC CWIS Illinois Intergenerational Initiative: http://www.siu.edu/offices/iii/

Center for the Study of Aging: http://www.rand.org/centers/aging/

Children

Child Welfare Home Page: http://www.childwelfare.com/
Administration for Children & Families: http://www.acf.dhhs.gov/
National Center for Children in Poverty: http://cait.cpmc.columbia.edu/dept/nccp/
National Child Rights Alliance: http://www.ncra-youthrights.org/
Global ChildNet: http://edie.cprost.sfu.ca/gcnet/index.html
Child Sexual Abuse: http://www.commnet.edu/QVCTC/student/LindaCain/sexabuse.html
Child Abuse: Statistics, Research, & Resources: http://www.jimhopper.com/abstats
No Safe Place: Children and Violence: http://www.oseda.missouri.edu/kidcnt/reports/violence/
The American Association of Open Adoption Agencies: http://www.openadoption.org/
Safety nets for children are weakest in US: http://www.unicef.org/pon96/indust4.htm
Contract with America's Children: http://www.childrennow.org

Conflict Resolution & Non-Violence

Fellowship of Reconciliation: http://www.nonviolence.org/~nvweb/for/
The Nonviolence Web: http://www.netaxs.com/~nvweb/
Conflict Home Page: http://www.igc.org/igc/gateway/pnindex.html

Disabilities

ADA Information Center On-Line Home Page: http://adabbs.hr.state.ks.us/dc/
The Disability Rights Activist: http://www.teleport.com/~abarhydt/
Yahoo!-Society & Culture: Disabilities:
       http://www.yahoo.com/Society_and_Culture/Disabilities/
American Foundation for the Blind: http://www.afb.org/afb/
The ARC, a national organization on mental retardation: http://TheArc.org/welcome.html
Ability Index: http://www.ability.org.uk/

Economic Policy

Links

free-Market.net: A Starting Point for Liberty on the Internet: http://www.free-market.net/
Internet Resources for Economists: http://www.ssc.upenn.edu/econ/Econ-Resources.html

Resources & Organizations

CAC: Welcome to the Citizen Advocacy Center: http://www.essential.org/cac/

Center for Insurance Research (CIR) Home Page: http://www.essential.org/orgs/cir/
The Taxpayer Assets Project: http://www.tap.org/
CPSR's Home Page: http://www.cpsr.org
Citizens Trust Home Page: http://www.efund.com/

Economic Policy Institutes & Projects (Governmental & Nongovernmental)

Bureau of Labor Statistics: http://stats.bls.gov/blshome.htm
U.S. Department of Labor: http://www.dol.gov/
National Bureau of Economic Research:
    http://www.fred.ifas.ufl.edu/resources/node75.html#SECTION000142000000000000000
BLS Home Page: http://stats.bls.gov:80/datahome.htm
The Center for Economic Conversion: http://www.conversion.org/
The Competitive Enterprise Institute: http://www.CEI.org/
World Resources Institute (WRI) Home page: http://www.wri.org/

Environment

Links

Environmental Organizations: http://envirolink.org/orgs/index.html
Environmental Organization Web Directory: http://www.webdirectory.com/
The Environmental Resources Information Network: http://www.tap.org/erin/
EcoNet Home Page: http://www.igc.org/igc/gateway/enindex.html

Organizations

Nationwide Green Org's in the USA.: http://www.greens.org/forums/agree.html
U.S. National Green Program: http://www.greens.org/gpusa/program.html
Greenpeace International Home Page: http://www.greenpeace.org/
Friends of the Earth: http://www.foe.org/
Sierra Club: http://www.sierraclub.org
Zero Population Growth: http://www.zpg.org
World Conservation Monitoring Centre: http://www.wcmc.org.uk/
Citizens Clearinghouse for Hazardous Waste: http://www.chej.org
Nautilis Institute: http://www.nautilus.org/
NIRS Web Site: http://www.nirs.org/
Ozone Action WWW Server: http://www.ozone.org/
The Earth Times: http://earthtimes.org/
PRAXIS: http://caster.ssw.upenn.edu/~restes/praxis.html
WorldWatch Home Page: http://www.worldwatch.org/

Food Policy

The HungerWeb: http://www.brown.edu/Departments/World_Hunger_Program/
The Hunger Project - Web Page: http://www.igc.org/thp/
Food for the Hungry: World Crisis Network: http://www.fh.org/
Northwest Harvest: http://www.northwestharvest.org/
Farmers Co-op Association: http://www.me.uwyo.edu/man-docs/WY/WY.940813205501.html
Taste of the Nation: http://www.strength.org
USDA's Home Page: http://www.usda.gov/
USDA-National Agricultural Statistics Service Home Page: http://www.usda.gov/nass/
American Farmland Trust's Home Page: http://www.farmland.org
Rural Development, USDA: http://www.rurdev.usda.gov

Gays & Lesbians

Links

Klaver's Cool Queer Connections: http://huizen.dds.nl/~klaver/index2.html
Queer Links: http://www.zoom.com/personal/staci/queer.htm

Resources & Organizations

Stonewall Revisited: http://www.stonewallrevisited.com/
National Gay & Lesbian Task Force: http://www.ngltf.org/
League of Gay & Lesbian Voters: http://www.lglv.org
And Justice for All: http://www.qrd.org/qrd/www/orgs/aja/
NLPAC: http://www.nlpac.org
NOW & Lesbian Rights: http://now.org/now/issues/lgbi/lgbi.html
FeMiNa-Lesbians: http://www.femina.com
Yoohoo! Lesbians!: http://www.sappho.com
United Lesbians of African Heritage: http://members.aol.com/uloah/home.html
Lesbian Mothers Support Society: http://www.lesbian.org/lesbian-moms/
Lesbian History Project (in Southern California): http://www-lib.usc.edu/~retter/main.html
NGLTF Youth Institute: http://www.youth.org/loco/ngltfyi/
Youth Assistance Organization/Youth Action Online: http://youth.org/
Out.com - #1 Gay/Lesbian Web Site!: http://www.out.com
Qworld (Gay & Lesbian): http://www.qworld.org/
Internections: The Internet Company: http://www.imageplaza.com/

Gender Issues

Women

Links

WomensNet@igc: http://www.igc.org/igc/gateway/wnindex.html
Femina: http://www.femina.com/
Feminist Activist Resources on the Net: http://www.igc.apc.org/women/feminist.html
FMF - Feminist Gateway: http://www.feminist.org/gateway/1_gatway.html
Gender-Related Electronic Forums: http://www-unix.umbc.edu/~korenman/wmst/forums.html
Feminist Activist Resources on the Net: Sexual Harassment & Rape Resources:
    http://www.igc.apc.org/women/activist/harass.html

Resources & Organizations

NOW (National Organization for Women): http://www.now.org/
Feminist Majority Foundation: http://www.feminist.org/
VOWworld: Voices of Women: http://www.voiceofwomen.com/
Women Leaders Online: http://wlo.org/
Center for the American Woman and Politics: http://www.rci.rutgers.edu/~cawp/
Caltech Women's Center: http://www.cco.caltech.edu/~wcenter/
Women's Resource Center: http://www.nd.edu/~wrc/
Heartless Bitches International-"Deal With It!": http://www.heartless-bitches.com/
The Cybergrrl Webstation - Welcome: http://www.cybergrrl.com/
Making Sense: A Resource for Understanding Women's Health: http://www.ppca.org
Welcome to the Andrea Dworkin Web Site!: http://www.igc.org/Womensnet/dworkin/
Washington Feminist Faxnet (WFF): http://www.feminist.com/ffn.htm

Violence, Sexual Abuse & Survivors

The Family Violence Prevention Fund: http://www.fvpf.org
Yahoo!-Society & Culture: Crimes: Domestic Violence: Organizations:
    http://dir.yahoo.com/Society_and_Culture/Crime/Types_of_Crime/Domestic_Violence/O
    rganizations/
Domestic Violence Home page: http://www.feminist.org/other/dv/dvhome.html
Sexual Assault Information Page: http://www.cs.utk.edu/~bartley/saInfoPage.html
Kathy's Essential Information on Abuse, Assault, Rape, & Domestic Violence:
    http://www.mcs.net/~kathyw/abuse.html
Victims of Incest Can Emerge Survivors (VOICES) in Action, Inc.:
    http://www.voices-action.org/

Men's Issues
Index Page: The Backlash: http://www.backlash.com/

Government: Agencies, Legislative Parties, Information and Reform

Links & References

Thomas: Legislative Information on the Internet: http://thomas.loc.gov/
FedWorld:
    http://www.fred.ifas.ufl.edu/resources/node19.html#SECTION00063000000000000000
The Political Network: http://www.polinet.com/
Federal Budget Primer: http://www.vote-smart.org/
Terry's Political Page: http://www.mebbs.com/tenny/politics.htm
United States of America (!): http://www.politicalresources.net/usa1.htm
The Texas Political Resource Page-Presented by George Strong & Associates:
    http://www.political.com/
Congressional Voting Record Sampler: http://www.vote-smart.org/
PRAG Page: http://www.luc.edu/depts/curl/prag/
Bad Subjects: Political Education for Everyday Life: http://eserver.org/bs/
NCSL State-Federal Relations and Policies: http://www.ncsl.org/statefed/afipolcy.htm#welfare

Federal Government Offices, Agencies, and Legislative Bodies:

Links

Federal Government Resources on the Web:
    http://www.lib.umich.edu/libhome/Documents.center/federal.html
U.S. Government Resources: http://remus.rutgers.edu/~rhoads/Commission/entitlement.html
Independent Federal Agencies and Commissions:
    http://www1.whitehouse.gov/WH/Independent_Agencies/html/independent_links.html

Government Agencies

GAO Home Page: http://www.gao.gov/
Department of Veteran Affairs: http://www.va.gov/
Homepage: U.S. Department of Health & Human Services: http://www.os.dhhs.gov/
SSA (Social Security Administration) Home Page: http://www.ssa.gov/

Welcome to GSA: http://www.gsa.gov/
U.S. Department of Education: http://www.ed.gov/
SSI: http://www.ssa.gov:80/programs/ssi/publications/ssi.html#PART 1
AmeriCorps: http://www.cns.gov/
GPO Access: http://www.access.gpo.gov/su_docs/index.html

Congress & The White House

The White House: http://www.whitehouse.gov
U.S. House of Representatives-Home Page: http://www.house.gov/
The United States Congress: http://www.vote-smart.org/
The United States Senate: http://www.senate.gov/
U.S. House of Representatives: gopher.house.gov
U.S. Senate: gopher.senate.gov

Political Parties

The Democratic Party: http://www.democrats.org
Republican National Committee - Republican Main Street!: http://www.rnc.org/
Green Parties of North America: http://www.greens.org/
Libertarian party: http://www.lp.org/
Socialist Party USA Cybercenter: http://sunsite.unc.edu/spc/index.html
The New Party: http://www.newparty.org
IWW (International Workers of the World): http://iww.org/
About the Communist Party, USA: http://www.hartford-hwp.com/cp-usa/docs/about.html

Political Organizations & Movements

Americans Against Political Corruption: http://www.essential.org
Turn Left . . . the Home of Liberalism: http://www.cjnetworks.com/~cubsfan/liberal.html
Congressional Accountability Project: http://www.essential.org/
The Center for Responsive Politics: http://www.vote-smart.org
The Perot Periodical Home Page: http://www.brainlink.com/~nota/
Democratic Leadership Council - Progressive Policy Institute: http://www.dlcppi.org/
Republican Party Links: ://www.mcn.org/1/elections/repub.html
Center for Public Integrity Home Page: http://www.essential.org/
CIVIX: http://ibert.org/
The Liberal Information Page: http://www.cjnetworks.com/~cubsfan/liberal.htmll
Communitarianism: http://www.cpn.org/sections/tools/models/communitarianism.html
Citizens Democracy Corps Home Page: http://www.cdc.org/

Health

National Institutes of Health (NIH) Home Page: http://www.nih.gov/
Centers for Disease Control and Prevention Home Page: http://www.cdc.gov/
American Public Health Association (APHA): http://www.apha.org/
National Health Information Center: http :// www.health.gov/NHIC
Health Services/Technology Assessment Text: http://text.nlm.nih.gov/
The USDOL OSHA Home Page: http://www.osha.gov/

he Body: A Multimedia AIDS & HIV (Information Resource: http://www.thebody.com/
MSO Managed Healthcare Forum: http://www.amso.com/
CHS : http://www.cdc.gov/nchs
ealth Index: http://www.usatoday.com/life/health/archive.htm
lobal Health - Key Resources: http://www.pitt.edu/HOME/GHNet/GHKR.html
he World Health Organization WWW Home Page: http://www.who.int/
merican Psychiatric Association: http://www.psych.org/
olicy.com - Health Care Forum: http://www.speakout.com/Activism/healthcare/
HCPR Home Page: http://www.ahcpr.gov/
ospital Web: http://neuro-www.mgh.harvard.edu/hospitalweb.shtml
overnment and International Organizations: http://mcfsun1.wustl.edu/library/medical/gov.html

ousing

.S. Department of Housing and Urban Development: http://www.hud.gov/
ational Coalition for the Homeless: http://nch.ari.net/
ome Page of Texas Low Income Housing Information
  ervice:http://www.texashousing.org/txlihis/index.html/
ousing Links:http: //www.texashousing.org/txlihis/index.html
irectory of State and National Homeless/Housing Organizations: http://nch.ari.net/direct1.html
abitat for Humanity International: http://www.habitat.org/
enter Households and Affordable Units:
       http://www.habitat.org/how/why.html
ffordable Housing for All?:
       http://www.habitat.org/how/why.html
he State of the Nation's Housing: Credits: http://www.nahb.com
ousing and Household Economic Indicators:
       http://www.census.gov/ftp/pub/hhes/www/index.html
merican Housing Survey: http://www.census.gov/ftp/pub/hhes/www/ahs.html
eattle's Homeless Newspaper: httphttp://www.realchangenews.org//
Yahoo! http://dir.yahoo.com/Society_and_Culture/Issues_and_Causes/Housing/Homelessness/

uman & Civil Rights

mnesty International-USA: http://www.amnesty-usa.org//
CLU Freedom Network: http://www.aclu.org/
yber-Rights Home Page: Other Web Sites:
       http://www.cpsr.org/cpsr/nii/cyber-rights/interesting-web-site.html
ahoo!-Business & Economy: Organizations: Public Interest Groups: Prison Rights
       http://dir.yahoo.com/Society_and_Culture/Crime/Correction_and_Rehabilitation/Issues//

nternational Policy

OECD Washington Center Home Page: http://www.oecdwash.org/
United States Information Service (USIA): http://usinfo.state.gov//
The World Bank Home Page: http://www.worldbank.org/
UNDP - United Nations Development Programme: http://www.undp.org/
Social Development: http://www.mennonitecc.ca
Multinational Monitor Online: http://www.essential.org/monitor/monitor.html
The Multinationals Resource Center http://www.essential.org/mrc
Actionaid Home Page: http://www.oneworld.org/actionaid/index.html
OneWorld Online Home Page: http://www.oneworld.org/
International Data Resources: http://dpls.dacc.wisc.edu/apdu/index.html
DPLS international Data Resources: http://dpls.dacc.wisc.edu/apdu/index.html
The Overseas Development Network: http://www.igc.apc.org/odn/index.html
WWW Virtual Library: Russian and East European Studies:http://www.ucis.pitt.edu/reesweb/
Center for Russian and East European studies:http://www.ucis.pitt.edu/crees/
African National Congress Home Page: http://www.anc.org.za/
UN Commission on Sustainable Development (CSD): gopher://gopher.un.org/11/esc/cn17
What is Sustainable Development?: http://www.census.gov/population/pop-profile/toc.html
Environment: Sustainable Development:http://usinfo.state.gov/
IGC Development: Internet-Resource Collection: http://www.igc.org/igc/issues/develop/or.html
Welcome to the Public Information Center: http://www.worldbank.org/html/pic/PIC.html
UNICEF Home Page: http://www.unicef.org/
IASSIST Workshop: Strategies for Locating and Using Internaitonal Data:
        http://dpls.dacc.wisc.edu/apdu/workbook_I.html
World Health Organization WWW Home Page: http://www.who.int/
Index of NGOs in Official Relations with WHO: http://www.who.int

Law & Social Policy
Center for Law and Social Policy : http://www.clasp.org
Internet Resources for Law & Social Policy: http://www.brynmawr.edu/library/Docs/law.html
The Center for Study of Responsive Law: http://www.csrl.org/
NAPIL Home Page: http://www.napil.org
Supreme Court Decisions: http://www.law.cornell.edu/supct/

Links to Policy-Oriented Web Sites

The Electronic Policy Network: http://epn.org/
Directory of Organizations: http://www.igc.org
Conte's Compendium -- Public Policy: http://world.std.com/~fconte/index.html
*Macrocosm USA's Central Links Station:
        http://www.macronet.org/macronet/newsites/links.html
Welcome to NAMINET: http://www.santafe.edu/~naminet/index.html

ahoo!-Social Science: http://www.yahoo.com/social_science

News & Media Sources:

Media Links

Welcome to the nando.net: http://www.nando.net/
Progressive Publications and News Services: http://www.igc.org/igc/gateway/news.html
Political Magazines and News: http://www.netcapitol.com
Yahoo Top Stories Summary: http://www.yahoo.com/headlines/news/
Newspapers on the World Wide Web: http://www.gt.kth.se/publishing/news.html
Netinfo: Access to Magazines: http://128.83.185.16/netinfo/magazines.html

Media Sources

Newspapers

The New York Times on the Web: http://www.nytimes.com/
Los Angeles Times Web Site: http://www.latimes.com/HOME/
Wall Street Journal Headlines: http://info.wsj.com
The Washington Times: http://www.AmericasNewspaper.com/
trib.com Home Page: http://www.trib.com/
TimesFax: http://nytimesfax.com/

Magazines

This week's Time Magazine: http://www.time.com
U.S. News Online: http://www.usnews.com/usnews/main.htm
National Review: http://www.townhall.com/nationalreview/
Mother Jones Magazine: http://www.mojones.com/mother_jones/mother_jones.html
Dollars and Sense Magazine: http://www.igc.apc.org/dollars/
Utne Online: http://www.utne.com/

Other Media Sources
EXTRA!– The Magazine of Fair : http://www.fair.org/extra/index.html
Online News Hour (National Public Radio): http://www.pbs.org/newshour/
CNN Interactive: http://www.cnn.com/
AP on the Globe Online: http://www.boston.com/globe/
Canada Newswire Ltd.: http://www.newswire.ca/
The On-Line Report of the Progressive Review:
        http://emporium.turnpike.net/P/ProRev/index.htm
The White House Briefing Room: http://www.whitehouse.gov/WH/html/briefroom.html#fsbr

Welcome to C-Span Networks: http://www.c-span.org/
Legi-Slate: News of the Day: http://www.legislate.com/n/news/961112.htm

Organizations
FAIR- Fairness and Accuracy in Reporting : http://www.fair.org
NewsPrints: http://www.essential.org/newsprints/newsprints.html
Media Access Project: http://www.mediaaccess.org/
AlterNet: http://www.igc.apc.org/an/

Non-Profit Organizations and Foundations

United Way: http://www.unitedway.org
America's Charities Homepage: http://www.charities.org/
Welcome to the Foundation Center: http://fdncenter.org/
Internet NonProfit Center-Information About Charity and Charities: http://www.nonprofits.org/
Nonprofit.net: http://www.nonprofit.net/
Yahoo!-Business & Economy Organizations: Foundations
         http://www.yahoo.com/Business_and_Economy/Organizations/
EFF Web-The Electronic Frontier Foundation: http://www.eff.org/
Monthly Review Foundation: http://www.monthlyreview.org

People of Color

Resources & Organizations

Virtual Community: Diversity & Ethnic Studies:
         http://www.public.iastate.edu/~savega/asian_am.htm
Yahoo! - Business and Economy: Organizations: Public Interest Groups: Minorities:
         http://www.yahoo.com/Business_and_Economy/Organizations/Public_Interest_Groups/
         Minorities/
Minority Affairs Forum: ftp://heather.cs.ucdavis.edu/pub/README.html
Equal Opportunity Publications: http://www.eop.com/
Diversity: http://latino.sscnet.ucla.edu/diversity1.html
National Association for Ethnic Studies: http://www.ksu.edu/ameth/naes/
Internet Resources for Urban/Minority Families:
         http://eric-web.tc.columbia.edu/families/other.html
ACF Programs: Department of Health and Human Services:
         http://www.acf.dhhs.gov/ACFPrograms/afdc/index.html
Urban/Minority Families: http://eric-web.tc.columbia.edu/families/
Affirmative Action Office: http://www.nau.edu/~affirm/

African Americans

AACP Online: http://www.naacp.org/
The National Urban League: http://www.nul.org/
African Americans:
>   http://www.fanniemae.com:8080/HousingResearch/PublishedRes/SubjectIndex/su_afrca
>   mer_cns.html
SA African American Newspapers and Publications: http://www.bnl.com/aasm/pubs.html
African American Home Ppage: http://www.lainet.com/~joejones/
Virtually Afrocentric: http://www.he.net/~awe/makheru.htm
African American Information: http://www.rain.org/~kmw/aa.html
Welcome to AfriNet: http://www.afrinet.org/
AfroNet Homepage: http://www.afronet.com/
Temple University's African-American Studies Dept. HomePage:
>   http://astro.ocis.temple.edu/~masante/
Freedom Journal Online: http://www.melanet.com
National Black Child Development Institute: http://www.nbcdi.org/
W.E.B. Dubois Institute: http://web-dubois.fas.harvard.edu/
National African Leadership Summit: http://www.melanet.com
KWANZAA Information Center: http://www.melanet.com
Black Population Profile: 1995:
>   http://www.census.gov

Hispanics

National Council of La Raza: http://www.nclr.org
LatinoLink Home Page: http://www.latinolink.com/
CLNET: http://latino.sscnet.ucla.edu/
Welcome to the Zone Zero: http://zonezero.com/
Hispanic Biz: http://www.hispanicbiz.com/facts.htm
Hispanics Against Liberal Takeover: http://www.pocho.com/varrio.html
NCLR Brochure: http://latino.sscnet.ucla.edu/community/nclr.html

Asian Americans

Asian American Resources:
http://www.mit.edu:8001/afs/athena.mit.edu/user/i/r/irie/www/aar.html
Alliance for Asian Rights and Empowerment: http://sun3.lib.uci.edu/~dtsang/awarefs.htm
Asian & Pacific Islander American Health Forum: http://www.apiahf.org

Native Americans

NativeWeb Home Page: http://www.nativeweb.org
NativeNet: http://niikaan.fdl.cc.mn.us/natnet/
Index of Native American Resources on the Net:
        http://hanksville.phast.umass.edu/misc/NAresources.html
Indian Health Service: http://www.tucson.ihs.gov/

Poverty

Poverty Institutes & Organization

Center on Budget and Policy Priorities: http://epn.org/cbpp.html
Institute for Research on Poverty: http://www.ssc.wisc.edu/irp/
Institute on Race and Poverty: http://www.umn.edu/law/centers/race-pov.htm
Welfare and Families (Idea Central): http://epn.org/idea/welfare.html

Poverty Resources

The Sticky Wicket: Poverty's Home Page -08/14/96:
        http://www2.ari.net/home/poverty/welcome.html
Poverty Research Briefs...: http://www.cdinet.com/Rockefeller/Briefs/brief2.htm
Poverty 1995: http://www.census.gov/ftp/pub/hhes/www/povty95.html
Income and Poverty: 1994 Income Summary:
        http://www.census.gov/ftp/pub/hhes/income/incsum.html
Income and Poverty: Poverty Summary: http://www.census.gov/pub/hhes/income/povsum.html
Income and Benefits Policy – Poverty Risk Factors : http://www.urban.org
50 Facts About Poverty: http://garnet.berkeley.edu:3333/faststats/povertystats.html
Poverty; Welfare; Ethics: http://www.acusd.edu/ethics/poverty.html
Poverty Areas: http://www.census.gov/pub/socdemo/www/povarea.html
ESA - The Minimum Wage: http://www.dol.gov/dol/esa/public/minwage/main.htm

Public Assistance

U.S. Department of Health and Human Services: http://www.dhhs.gov
American Public human Services Association: http://www.aphsa.org/
ACF's Welfare Reform Resource Page: http://www.acf.dhhs.gov/news/welfare/wr/
Normal Page: http://www.welfareinfo.org/
AFDC Overview - 1994 - Contents:
        http://www.acf.dhhs.gov/programs/afdc/reports/1994/overview/index.htm
Research: Resources for Social Policy

Publications

dget of the United States Government, FY 1997: http://www.doc.gov/BudgetFY97/index.html
verview of Entitlement Programs: Green Book: http://aspe.os.dhhs.gov/GB/gbpage.htm
brary of Congress Online Services: http://lcweb.loc.gov/homepage/online.html#locis
PO (U.S. Government Printing Office) Access: http://www.access.gpo.gov/
al--A-Book Public Policy Books-Listed by http://www.igc.org/igc/gateway/pnindex.html/
Mich Documents Center: http://www.lib.umich.edu/libhome/Documents.center/index.html
e Social Service Review: http://www.journals.uchicago.edu/SSR/
cus Magazine: http://www.ssc.wisc.edu/irp/focus/focus.htm
cent IRP Focus Articles: http://www.ssc.wisc.edu/irp/focus/focus.htm
NU-Register of Social Sci. E-Journals:
        http://coombs.anu.edu.au/CoombsHome.html
onomic Policy Institute Publications: http://www.lights.com/epi/index.html

her Resources

elcome to HandsNet: http://www.handsnet.org/
cial Science Information Gateway SOSIG: http://sosig.esrc.bris.ac.uk/
PLS -- Archival Online Repository: http://dpls.dacc.wisc.edu/archive.html
he Argus Clearinghouse: http://www.clearinghouse.net/
ther Archives and Social Science Information Services: http://dawww.essex.ac.uk/othserv.html
ational Longitudinal Surveys Home Page: http://psc.lsa.umich.edu/
CSD Data Collection: http://ssdc.ucsd.edu/
opulation Index: http://popindex.princeton.edu/
esearch: gopher://gsro.carleton.ca:413/11/ResearchRecorder/
enter for Survey Research:http://www.indiana.edu/~csr//
olitical Sciences Resources (Rutgers): http://www.rutgers.edu
olitical Sciences Resources on the Web:
tp://www.lib.umich.edu/libhome/Documents.center/polisci.html
conomic Resources on the Net: http://www.lib.umich.edu/libhome/rrs/classes/econ.html
OEcon WWW:http://darkwing.uoregon.edu/~econ/Econworld.html
.S. Census Bureau Home Page: http://www.census.gov/
ensus Data:
        http://www.fred.ifas.ufl.edu/resources/node20.html#SECTION00064000000000000000
tatistical Abstract of the U.S.:http://www.census.gov/statab/www//
ureau of Labor Statistics: http://stats.bls.gov/blshome.html
WT Database Welcome Page: http://cansim.epas.utoronto.ca:5680/pwt/pwt.html
he Panel Study of Income Dynamics: http://www.umich.edu/~psid/
conData:
        http://www.fred.ifas.ufl.edu/resources/node9.html#SECTION00054000000000000000
ational Trade Data Bank:
        http://www.fred.ifas.ufl.edu/resources/node24.html#SECTION00068000000000000000

Public Domain Financial Data:
        http://www.fred.ifas.ufl.edu/resources/node43.html#SECTION00085000000000000000
Regional Economic Information system, 1969-1994: http://www.lib.virginia.edu
Labor Force Statistics from the Current Population Survey: http://stats.bls.gov:80/cpshome.htm
STAT-USA/Internet Databases: http://www.stat-usa.gov/
Social Work

National Association of Social Workers: http://www.naswdc.org
Council on Social Work Education (CSWE): http://www.cswe.org/
National Association of Black Social Workers: http://www.nabsw.org/
Good Works: A Guide to Social Change Careers: http://www.essential.org/goodworks/
Welcome!!! The Social Worker Network: http://www.spring-board.com/two/SocialWorkerNet/
The New Social Worker Online:http://www.socialworker.com/
Yahoo!-Social Science: Social Work: http://www.yahoo.com/Social_Science/Social_Work/
Yahoo!-Social Science: Social Work: Organizations: Professional: National Association of
Social Workers:
        http://www.yahoo.com/Social_Science/Social_Work/Organizations/Professional/Nationa
        _Association_of_Social_Workers/
Selected Social Work Resources on the Web:
        http://www.lib.umich.edu/libhome/Social.lib/social.html
Social Work Library: http://www.usc.edu/Library/Soc/
Social Work Library Internet Class: http://www.lib.umich.edu/libhome/Social.lib/social.html
Social Work Cafe: http://www.geocities.com/Heartland/4862/swcafe.html

Stigma, Oppression, & Advocacy Organizations

Links to Progressive Advocacy Organizations:

PeaceNet Home Page:http://www.igc.org/igc/gateway/pnindex.html/
PeaceNet's Directory of Organizations:http://www.igc.org/igc/gt/PeaceNet/
Progressive People Links: http://www.people-link.org/
WebActive: http://www.webactive.org/
The Electronic Activist: http://www.berkshire.net/~ifas/activist/
The Progressive Directory @igc: http://www.igc.apc.org/index.html
IGC Information: http://www.igc.apc.org/igc/igcinfo.html
The Well: http://www.well.com/
Adam Rifkin's Activism Links Page: http://www.cs.caltech.edu/~adam/LEAD/active_links.html
John Lathrop's Launch Pad: http://www.elite.net/~lathropj/index.html

General Advocacy Organizations

People for the American Way: http://www.thebody.com/pfaw/pfawpage.html
Tenant Net Home Page: http://tenant.net/
Welcome to the Civic Network: http://www.civic.net/
Essential.ORG WWW Server: http://www.essential.org/
Alliance for Justice: http://www.afj.org/
Center for Science in the Public Interest: http://www.cspinet.org/cspi/
Public Citizen: http://www.citizen.org/

Progressive Professional Organizations

Physicians for Social Responsibility:http://www.psr.org//
Union of Concerned Scientists: http://www.ucsusa.org/
Physicians for a National Health Program: http://www.pnhp.org/

Conservative Web Sites & Groups

Christian Coalition Home Page: http://cc.org/
Rush to the Right Side....: http://www.rtside.com/
Committee for a Responsible Federal Budget:
        http://www.network-democracy.org/social-security/bb/whc/crfb.html
The Ronald Reagan Home Page:http://reagan.webteamone.com/
CCRKBA: http://www.CCRKBA.org:80/ccrkba.org/
NRTA.org (National Rifle Association) Home Page: http://www.nra.org/
NRLC Home Page: http://www.nrlc.org/
Acton Institute Online: http://www.acton.org/acton.html
GOPAC: http://www.gopac.com/
NTU Information Center: http://www.ntu.org
Town Hall - Explore the New Conservative World: http://townhall.com/

Community & Labor Groups

LaborNet@IGC Home Page: http://www.labornet.org//
The New Social Movements Network: http://www.interweb-tech.com/nsmnet/
Labor Policy Association: http://www.lpa.org/lpa/index.html
MassINC: http://www.massinc.org/
Californians for Justice: http://www.igc.apc.org/cfj/
ACORN Home Page:http://www.acorn.org/newsite1.htm
Welcome to AFSCME: http://www.afscme.org/
AFL-CIO Home Page: http://www.aflcio.org/
Holt Labor Library: http://www.holtlaborlibrary.org/
Labor/Community Strategy Center Home Page: http://www.igc.apc.org/lctr/

Jobs With Justice: http://www.igc.apc.org/jwj/

Substance Abuse

National Clearinghouse for Alcohol & Drug Information: http://www.health.org/
National Institute on Drug Abuse http://www.nida.nih.gov/
Substance Abuse and Mental Health Services Administration: http://www.samhsa.gov/
Join Together Online: http://www.jointogether.org/

Think Tanks & Public Policy

Links to Think Tanks

The Electronic Policy Network: http://epn.org/
State-Based Think Tanks: http://www.cascadepolicy.org/spn.htm
Thinklink: http://www.thinktank.com/thnklnk.html

Population Studies Institutes:

Population Studies Center-Univ of Michigan: http://www.psc.lsa.umich.edu/
Office of Population Research: http://opr.princeton.edu/
East-West Center Program on Population: http://www2.ewc.hawaii.edu/pop/pop50000.htm
Penn State Population Institute: http://www.pop.psu.edu/

Governmental/Public Policy Institutes:

UC Berkeley Institute of Governmental Studies: http://www.igs.berkeley.edu:8880/
Institute for the Study of Civic Values: http://libertynet.org/~edcivic/iscvhome.html
Institute for Policy Analysis: http://www.chass.utoronto.ca/ipa/
John F. Kennedy School of Government Home Page: http://www.ksg.harvard.edu
LBJ School of Public Affairs: Public Policy: http://www.utexas.edu/lbj/
Institute for First Amendment Studies: http://apocalypse.berkshire.net/~ifas/index.html
The Carter Center: http://www.cartercenter.org

.S. Institute for Peace: gopher://gopher.usip.igc.org:7001/1/
egislative Analyst's Office (California): http://www.lao.ca.gov/

hink-Tanks

merican Enterprise Institute (AEI): http://www.aei.org
rookings Institution: http://www.brook.edu/
ascade Policy Institute: http://www.CascadePolicy.org/
enter for Policy Research: http://www-cpr.maxwell.syr.edu/
laremont Institute: http://www.claremont.org/
emocratic Leadership Council - Progressive Policy Institute: http://www.dlcppi.org/
mployee Benefit Research Institute: http://www.ebri.org/
amilies USA Home Page: http://www.familiesusa.org
udson Institute: http://www.hudson.org
AND Home Page: http://www.rand.org/
eason Foundation: http://www.reason.org/
he Progress and Freedom Foundation: http://www.townhall.com/pff/
he Aspen Institute Home Page: http://www.aspeninst.org/
he Heartland Institute: http://www.heartland.org/
he Heritage Foundation: http://www.heritage.org/
he Official CATO Institute Homepage: http://www.cato.org/
he Urban Institute Home Page: http://www.urban.org/
he Center for Voting and Democracy: http://www.igc.org/cvd/
he Independent Institute: http://Independent.org/
he Jerome Levy Economics Institute of Bard College: http://www.levy.org/
wentieth Century Fund: http://www.tcf.org
Welcome to NCPA: http://www.public-policy.org/~ncpa/

GLOSSARY

A

Access Privileges: The right to access and make changes to Web sites or Web pages. It also refers to having access to change or modify networks.

Address: The address assigned to a storage file, a device in a system or network, or any other data source on a network. This can also refer to an e-mail or WWW address.

B

Bandwidth: Measurement of how much information can be transmitted at a given time. The broader the bandwidth the more data can flow across the lines.

Baud: Measure of the data transmission speed of a telephone or network.

Bit: The smallest amount of information that can be transmitted.

Bookmarks: A way of storing pointers to Web sites in your browser.

Bottleneck: A system constraint that may reduce the speed and flow of communications, often during peak conditions.

BPS (bits per second): The measure of a modem's speed. See "Baud."

BBS (bulletin board system): An electronic bulletin board where users can leave messages or upload and download files or images. A BBS is also a dial-in service that provides information on specific topics. Many community BBS's offer Internet services.

Browser: An application that displays Web pages on your computer. Most web browsers also allow you to copy and print material from the Web, and access other Internet protocols such as e-mail, Gopher, news, and file transfers.

C

Carrier: A telecommunications provider which owns network switch equipment.

Common Carrier: A carrier that defines itself as serving the public.

Chat: A term used to describe real-time (live) conferencing. Users in a virtual "room" type out messages to one another on the keyboard.

Client/Server: The relationship between programs running on separate machines in a computer network. The server provides the services while the client uses them.

Communication Link: A system of hardware and software connecting two end users.

Compression/Decompression: A method of encoding/decoding that allows the transmission or storage of more information than a specific media (e.g., hard disk drive) could otherwise support.

Cyberspace: Refers to various forms of computer-related communication.

Database: A collection of information that is systematically organized and classified.

Dedicated Line: A private telecommunications phone line that is leased from a telecommunications carrier.

Download: To transfer data, programs or images *from* a remote computer or network *to* your PC or network.

FAQ (Frequently Asked Questions): List of questions and answers on a specific topic.

File Server: A computer that provides access to files for remote users or those on a network.

Flame War: A heated and emotional online debate.

FTP (File Transfer Protocol): The Internet protocol that allows the viewing, downloading, and uploading of files on remote computers. FTP lets users download files from a computer or network on the Internet to a PC or another network. Users can also transfer their own files to other computer systems. One common use of FTP is to download software from public sites.

Gateway: A node that connects compatible or incompatible networks.

GIF (Graphics Interchange Format): A format for image files. GIF file formats use a compression method to make files smaller.

Gopher: A browsing and searching protocol that lets you find and retrieve text and files i public databases.

H

Home Page: The WWW page that the user starts in. This page is also used as a base for Net searches.

HTML (Hyper Text Markup Language): A language in which Web pages are formatted and Web information is distributed. It is the standard for adding tags to a text file so that the file can be interpreted by a web browser.

HTML Editor: A program that allows you to add HTML tags to a text file.

HTTP (hypertext transfer protocol): The method by which documents are transferred from the host computer or server to browsers and individual users. It is the protocol that lets We servers and browsers communicate with each other.

Hyperlink: Connections between one piece of information (or Web site) and another. Specifically, hyperlinks (links) are an emphasized word or a phrase in a hypertext document that acts as a pointer to related information. Links are usually underlined and are a different color tha the rest of the text.

Hypermedia: A way of presenting information that is connected by links. This information may be presented using such media as text, graphics, audio, video, animation, or images.

Hypertext: Online navigation for the WWW. Hyperlinks (i.e., URLs) embedded in words or phrases allow users to select text, graphic images, or buttons which display related informatio or multimedia material.

I

Icon: A graphic representation (visual symbol) of an object, idea or function.

Information Superhighway: Generally thought of as the Internet and allied communications technologies. More specifically, it refers to the Clinton administration's plan to deregulate communication services, thereby allowing for the integration of the Internet, cable television, telephone services, business, entertainment, information providers, and education int one system. The goal is to provide a large network for information and entertainment.

IP Address: The Internet protocol address assigned to a host computer. This is the number that identifies your machine as unique on the Internet.

IRC (Internet Relay Chat): Like a CB radio, IRC lets you join a channel and converse with other people in real-time. See chat.

ISDN (Integrated Services Digital Network): A standard for high-speed transmission of simultaneous voice, data and video information. Using a special phone line, ISDN is generally faster than a normal phone connection.

ISP (Internet Service Provider): A company that provides dial-in access to the Internet. This can be on a fee for service basis (e.g., a commercial provider like AT&T, IBM, MCI, etc.) or free as in FreeNet and a university-based dial-in service.

Java: Known as applets, Java programs are embedded in HTML pages using a special tag. The browser automatically loads and executes the applet. Java allows functions to be executed almost immediately upon loading a HTML page (e.g., a series of sound files, etc.).

JPEG (or JPG) (Joint Photographic Experts Group): The most popular method for compressing photographic images. Many graphic files are in JPEG or JPG format and many web browsers accept it as a file format for viewing graphics.

L

Link: (See Hyperlink).

Listserv: E-mail mailing lists which allow for posting, reading, and downloading of messages. Can function somewhat like an electronic bulletin board.

M

MIDI (Musical Instrument Digital Interface): A standard that lets electronic musical devices communicate with each other.

MIME (Multipurpose Internet Mail Extension): Often an addendum to e-mail, MIME extensions identify the transmittal of non-text data files like movies, video, and graphics. MIME is also used for sending addendums to e-mail such as formatted documents, etc.

Modem (MODulator-DEModulator): Hardware that lets digital data be transmitted over phone lines.

MPEG (Moving Pictures Expert Group): A standard to compress full-motion video.

Multimedia: Computers that integrate audio, video and data.

N

Network: A system of interconnected computers that provide local or remote communications (e.g., voice, video, data, etc.). Networks facilitate the exchange of information between users with common interests.

P

PKZIP: A shareware compression utility for PCs.

PKUNZIP: Downloaded with PKZIP, PKKUNZIP is used to decompress files compressed with PKZIP.

Pointer: A URL address embedded in a Web page that points to the location of data in another record or file. A hyperlink is an example of a pointer.

"POP" (Point of Presence): An Internet service provider's dial-up connection for modem users. It is used to describe local connections so modem users don't have to dial long distance.

PPP (Point to Point Protocol): Dial-up Internet connection.

R

Real Time: The transmission and processing of events or transactions as they are actually occurring.

Robots: Programs which travel the Web looking for information (e.g., for indexing a search engine or to find errors in Web sites).

Router: A special machine that runs various protocols to direct network packets. Routers hold the Internet together.

S

Server: (See Client/Server): A host data station (e.g., a network) that provides facilities to terminals or other stations.

SGML (Standard Generalized Markup Language): A language used for describing other document languages. For example, HTML is defined using SGML.

Shareware: Software distributed on a "try and buy if you like" basis. Shareware can be downloaded directly from the Net or through a BBS. If you use the software after a specified period of time, you are expected to purchase it.

SLIP (Serial Line Internet Protocol): Dial-up Internet connection speaking in TCP/IP protocol. This is somewhat slower than a PPP protocol.

SSL: The Secure Socket Layer is a protocol that Netscape uses to provide people with secure transactions over the WWW.

TCP/IP (Transmission Control Protocol/Internet Protocol): The standard network communications protocol used to connect computer systems across the Internet.

Telnet: A network program that offers a way to log into and work from another computer.

UNZIP: To unzip a file means to decompress (expand) a file that has been compressed by a utility like PKZIP.

URL (Uniform Resource Locator): The site address with the name of the server, the file's directory path, and its file name. It is the location of a resource on the Internet. For example, the URL address for Harper Collins publishers is: http://www.harpercollins.com

Usenet (USEer Network): Subject-specific discussion forums stored on remote computers. This refers to newsgroups on the Internet.

VRML (Virtual Reality Modeling Language): A language in which Web pages are formatted so that they can support 3D graphics and spatially-based navigation.

WAIS (Wide Area Information Server): A powerful system for quickly searching through large amounts of information over the Internet.

WAV: The file extension used on some types of audio files.

Web Browser: Software that gives the user a graphical interface for searching, finding, viewing, and managing information on the WWW.

Web Page: A hypermedia document on the Web.

Web Site: Address of a server on the Internet.
Webmaster/Webmistress: System operator for a Web site.

WWW (World Wide Web): Internet system for world-wide hypertext linking. Describes the nature of the system of hypertext that marks the Web. Hypertext creates a "web" connections.

Z

ZIP: Compression of a file using PKZIP. The resulting file is called a "zip" file and usually ends with the extension ".zip".